RILKE

Duino Elegies

RAINER MARIA RILKE

Duino Elegies

WITH ENGLISH TRANSLATIONS BY
C. F. MacIntyre

UNIVERSITY OF CALIFORNIA PRESS
BERKELEY AND LOS ANGELES
1968

To Mr. James Callahan

I wish to dedicate these translations in acknowledgment of his help with the Sonnets to Orpheus.

C.F.M.

University of California Press
Berkeley and Los Angeles, California

© 1961 by C. F. MacIntyre

Fourth Printing, 1968

Library of Congress Catalog Card Number: 61-11876

Designed by Adrian Wilson

Manufactured in the United States of America

Introduction

The Elegies were begun at the castle of Duino, near Trieste, in 1912. The manuscript was carried through Spain, France, and Germany, and the poems as they now appear were finally completed at the Château Muzot, in Switzerland, in 1922.

They represent the culmination of Rilke's efforts to use his experience not as self-expression but as something more universal. They are neither simple, particularly lucid, nor passionate in a personal sense. The poet had developed beyond his earlier Romantic style in which he wrote of his emotions; he had created the "Thing-poems" of *Neue Gedichte*, which are almost purely objective; and in *Malte* he had rid himself of certain morbid fears, obsessions, and leanings toward the macabre. He had learned that poetry is the result of experiences rather than of feelings. Thus the Elegies present the matured evaluations of a man who had suffered greatly, so much that he finally overcame any desire to bemoan his fate or to accuse destiny; he had won a serenity from which he could regard death as the consummation and continuance of life, as the fullest and most real part of man's existence. Here are no blessed assurances of rewards, no tabulated proscriptions; the reader is dealing with Rilke's version of the process of becoming, through the evolution of a "wise passiveness," which, after a trial period of lamentation and suffering, can accept the next life. This is represented as no Grecian Elysium, no Hebraic or Catholic heaven, for here also pain is the lot of man. But there is this difference: after the drab state of becoming, man enters into a state ready for actual being in which he can acclaim the part played by sorrow in his evolution. This acceptance of sorrow and man's duty to praise it are major Rilkean themes. Man herewith becomes a Yea-sayer and is ready for the personal death implicit from the beginning.

I have read, made précis of, and rewritten several explanations of these poems, and I had originally intended to prepare a completely documented and scholarly introduction. But I have finally decided that none of them said anything Rilke had not already written more perfectly and clearly himself. A second reading of the series is certainly more valuable than pages of notes and supposed explanations. (With the *Sonnets to Orpheus* the situation is very different, and I have dealt with them accordingly.)

But the initial impact on the reader will undoubtedly be confusing, and a brief outline of the ten elegies may be helpful. The principal symbols —props, one might almost call them—are the angels, the heroes, the great lovers (always women), the mothers, the children who died young, the mime and doll, the acrobats, the animals and finally, the Laments, the personified sorrows of life. The Things:

trees, pitchers, tools, houses, stars, flowers, birds, et cetera, are minor supernumeraries.

Man has always attempted to establish himself on this fickle ball of earth. He can believe in such forces of nature as he has actually conquered. These are tangible. But other values, such as God, faith, and love—these so-called "spiritual values"—are only partially believed in. Eventually man must learn that his agonies and sufferings—certainly tangible and real enough—are his only riches. Yet in his weakness and isolation he naturally turns to things outside himself for help, and a summary of these is the theme of the introductory elegy.

FIRST ELEGY: "Whom can man use?" the poet asks himself. The angels are too terrible and aloof; man is no help to his fellow; even the animals recognize that he is a stranger here. Maybe a tree, one's home street, or an old habit or the night can help some. Then Rilke discusses the part of the great lovers (usually deserted women), whom, he insists, it is the poet's duty to praise. Saints and heroes are too intent on their destiny to avail man. The children who died young, "gently weaned from earthly things," no longer need him. Everything seems to stand alone; there is no help. But each of these themes will recur and be evaluated in the other elegies. For the present, the poet leaves man with the one consolation of music, a "blessed advancement" born from grief, according to the Greek story of Linos.

SECOND ELEGY: Angels, perhaps, were helpful in the days of the Old Testament, but Rilke maintained that his angels are rather those of Islam. The approach of such a being nowadays would kill the beholder. Man constantly breathes himself into and dissolves in cosmic space. The essence of the transitory, he has no proof of existence past death; even the lovers cannot believe that their tremendous feelings have any real eternity. We lack the classic restraint of the Greeks and can no longer behold in the gods symbols by means of which the heart might "temper itself more loftily."

THIRD ELEGY: Man's love is controlled by his dark inherited bloodstream; it is an impulsive, irrational thing incapable of devotion and of satisfying a woman's love. There is a fine eulogy of mother love, birth, and infancy—the treatment is tender without being sentimental. As the youth grows into manhood he becomes aware of his heritage from the past and his place in the continued history of the race. As usual, Rilke calls on the girls to aid, comfort, and restrain man.

FOURTH ELEGY: Ever since Goethe's puppet stage, Heinrich von Kleist's essay on dolls, and Eudo Mason's long chapter in his book, a good deal of nonsense has been written about dolls. Rilke dismisses the masked mime as a mere imitation of something and defends the doll, animated by the angel, as a more real symbol. There is nothing at all in the elegy which is difficult to understand. Man sits before the stage, the puppet show of life. The essence of the play is Parting, loss of those dear to us. Man must learn to accept death calmly. The faint picture of the poet's father is one of the finest passages in the series. The "boy with brown squint-eyes" is his cousin Egon, who is mentioned also in the Sonnets.

FIFTH ELEGY: This is one of the most impressive

and clearest, a halfway point. The acrobats from Picasso's picture are used as symbols of man's pitiful attempts to perform his part in life. It has been suggested that the little girl represents Rilke's pathetic picture of himself in childhood when his mother dressed and treated him as a girl. The ring of spectators around the acrobats, that "rose of gazing" which is ever blooming and losing its petals as people come and are bored and go away, is a fine figure. Man is both actor and spectator, almost the "blow and the wound" of Baudelaire. Then Rilke asks the angel for some supermundane help: a practicing ground where human actions might perhaps be perfected so that they could win the approbation of the "innumerable silent dead," who presumably have come into some higher wisdom in their state of being.

SIXTH ELEGY: The fig tree flowers modestly in the cavity of the green carapace—so to speak, it "skips over the blooming"; but man, who likes to linger and blossom, to live and enjoy the beautiful play before the serious part of life begins, retards his development as fruit, that is, as in death. The single-minded hero, however, a man of action who knows exactly what he was sent here to do, lives dangerously, and presses ever onward toward self-destruction (sacrifice for his cause), and the beginning of the next, the true part of life. Here is a strange physiological fertility rite in which the hero-sperm has it all his own way. Once born, the hero lets nothing hinder him, even love. He is already beyond all temporal distractions; he is ready to go into the "open" of his destiny.

SEVENTH ELEGY: This begins with a wooing song,

"pure as a bird's." Not only the beloved, but all girls, even the fallen and the dead, are petitioned to come. Life is glorious, but the outer world is constantly dwindling. While the *Zeitgeist* is creating vast storehouses of power, the temples are forgotten. (This is also a theme developed in the Sonnets.) The angel is addressed almost in a defiant tone. The poet will not woo him, but he cites architecture, music, and love as results of man's endeavor to praise something secure amid the flux of existence. The human hand (reminiscent of those carved by Rodin) remains wide open between the poet and the angel, "as safeguard and warning." The angel is unseizable, but the poet also does not intend to be taken tamely.

EIGHTH ELEGY: This is the most pessimistic of the lot. Animals know nothing about death and walk calmly into eternity, without fear. Their gaze is forward. The dead are already in the "open." Children touch upon it sometimes in their reveries and sleep. Lovers almost approach it, but are blocked off by each other. Birth itself, as a departure from the protected existence in the womb, is an agony. Man is always aware of fate and death, and lives ever bidding adieu.

NINTH ELEGY: Why, then, if one might undergo some strange metamorphosis into a laurel, as did Daphne, why does man cling so to life and attempt to evade his destiny, in death? Vastly he loves this world of Things, but what will he be able to take with him into "the other realm"? Human experience would have no voice there. Life is the time of the utterable, therefore let us praise while and what we can, even the simple tools that have beauty of form and live because of us. Possibly we may take the sufferings and experiences in love with us, but we must give ourselves confidently to earth's "sacred revelation . . . intimate death." Rilke had the odd notion that earth is resurrected "invisibly" in the transformation which man undergoes in death.

TENTH ELEGY: At the end of life, man begins to see the purpose of his nights of affliction. He has been a "spendthrift of sorrow" and has not put it to its use as a stimulus for praise. Henceforth he must "sing out jubilation and praise to the affirmative angels." Now Rilke comes to the magnificent description of the allegorical City of Pain, much more succintly done than Bunyan's or Thackeray's cities. His most trenchant irony and his rarely used humor are very effective, and a contrast is prepared for the lofty dignity of the Land of Lamentation into which the dead man is now led. Here he continues "to live" on in a beautiful elegiac atmosphere where his companions are personifications of the Sorrows. In a landscape which is reminiscent of Egypt, the individual goes on learning under new constellations. He sees the slender fountainhead of the River of Joy, a navigable river in the world of men. Finally his guide embraces him, weeping. And he disappears alone in two fine lines:

Lonely, he climbs the mountains of primeval pain.
And never once does his footstep ring from this
    soundless doom.

If the dead were able to communicate anything of their happiness, it would be to point at the catkins on the leafless hazel, or to the rain of early spring as it falls on the black earth. These are cheerful omens of better things to come. The last four lines are quite difficult and seem to mean that a falling (dying) thing is to be interpreted in terms of the "rising" happiness it can then enter.

Indubitably the *Duino Elegies* will take their place among the great and unforgettable poetry of the world. Their philosophy is borrowed from various sources, too obvious to tabulate. The unrhymed verses, varying considerably in length and texture, afford continually new interest. Although the style, sentence structure, grammar, and punctuation are arbitrary and often irritating, even controversial, their unraveling is worthwhile.

I want to express my debt of gratitude to many persons, several of whom have asked to remain unnamed (probably because they do not wish to shoulder the blame of my mistakes). Professor B. Q. Morgan of Stanford University made me do these translations three times—bless him!—and helped me with valuable suggestions, and M. Peter Paret has unstintingly given me time and advice. Finally a translator must attempt to fuse the whole into himself and give back something in his own language that he fondly believes may give an experience similar to that produced by a reading of the original. But a translation is always a petard for its maker.

C. F. M.

Weimar, San Francisco, Guadalajara,
Frankfort, Wiesbaden, Paris
1938–1960

Die Erste Elegie

Wer, wenn ich schriee, hörte mich denn aus der Engel
Ordnungen? und gesetzt selbst, es nähme
einer mich plötzlich ans Herz: ich verginge von seinem
stärkeren Dasein. Denn das Schöne ist nichts
als des Schrecklichen Anfang, den wir noch grade
    ertragen,
und wir bewundern es so, weil es gelassen verschmäht,
uns zu zerstören. Ein jeder Engel ist schrecklich.
Und so verhalt ich mich denn und verschlucke den
    Lockruf
dunkelen Schluchzens. Ach, wen vermögen
wir denn zu brauchen? Engel nicht, Menschen nicht,
und die findigen Tiere merken es schon,
daß wir nicht sehr verläßlich zu Haus sind
in der gedeuteten Welt. Es bleibt uns vielleicht
irgendein Baum an dem Abhang, daß wir ihn täglich
wiedersähen; es bleibt uns die Straße von gestern
und das verzogene Treusein einer Gewohnheit,
der es bei uns gefiel, und so blieb sie und ging nicht.

The First Elegy

Who, if I shouted, among the hierarchy of angels
would hear me? And supposing one of them
took me suddenly to his heart, I would perish
before his stronger existence. For beauty is nothing
but the beginning of terror we can just barely endure,
and we admire it so because it calmly disdains
to destroy us. Every angel is terrible.
And so I restrain myself and swallow the luring call
of dark sobbing. Ah, whom can we use then?
Not angels, not men, and the shrewd animals
notice that we're not very much at home
in the world we've expounded. Maybe on the hill-slope
some tree or other remains for us, so that
we see it every day; yesterday's street is left us,
and the gnarled fidelity of an old habit
that was comfortable with us and never wanted to leave.

O und die Nacht, die Nacht, wenn der Wind voller Weltraum
    Weltraum
uns am Angesicht zehrt—, wem bliebe sie nicht, die ersehnte,
    ersehnte,
sanft enttäuschende, welche dem einzelnen Herzen
mühsam bevorsteht. Ist sie den Liebenden leichter?
Ach, sie verdecken sich nur miteinander ihr Los.
Weißt du's *noch* nicht? Wirf aus den Armen die Leere
zu den Räumen hinzu, die wir atmen; vielleicht daß die Vögel
    die Vögel
die erweiterte Luft fühlen mit innigerm Flug.

Ja, die Frühlinge brauchten dich wohl. Es muteten manche
    manche
Sterne dir zu, daß du sie spürtest. Es hob
sich eine Woge heran im Vergangenen, oder
da du vorüberkamst am geöffneten Fenster,
gab eine Geige sich hin. Das alles war Auftrag.
Aber bewältigtest du's? Warst du nicht immer
noch von Erwartung zerstreut, als kündigte alles
eine Geliebte dir an? (Wo willst du sie bergen,
da doch die großen fremden Gedanken bei dir
aus und ein gehn und öfters bleiben bei Nacht.)
Sehnt es dich aber, so singe die Liebenden; lange
noch nicht unsterblich genug ist ihr berühmtes Gefühl.
Jene, du neidest sie fast, Verlassenen, die du
so viel liebender fandst als die Gestillten. Beginn
immer von neuem die nie zu erreichende Preisung;
denk: es erhält sich der Held, selbst der Untergang war ihm
    war ihm
nur ein Vorwand, zu sein: seine letzte Geburt.
Aber die Liebenden nimmt die erschöpfte Natur

Oh, and the night, the night, when the wind full
     of welkin
feeds on our faces—for whom wouldn't it stay,
yearned-for, gently disappointing night
that wearily confronts the solitary heart?
Is night more easy on lovers? Ah, they only
hide their fate from themselves by using each other.
Don't you know that *yet*? Throw the emptiness
     from your arms
into the spaces we breathe, so maybe the birds
can feel the expanded air, more ardently flying.

Yes, the springs needed you. And many stars
expected you to feel them. A wave rose
toward you in the past; or as you walked by
an open window, a violin yielded itself to someone.
All this was assignment. But could you handle it?
Weren't you always distraught by anticipation,
as if all this announced a sweetheart's coming?
(Where do you think you can hide her,
what with those great strange thoughts running in
     and out
of you and often staying for the night?)
But when you yearn, then sing of the girls who
     were lovers:
the fame of their passion has not been made
     immortal enough.
Those you almost envy, the deserted ones you found
so much more loving than those who had been
     appeased.
Ever newly begin the praise you cannot accomplish.
Remember: the hero keeps going, and even his ruin
was only a subterfuge for achieving his final birth.
But nature, exhausted, takes the lovers back

in sich zurück, als wären nicht zweimal die Kräfte,
dieses zu leisten. Hast du der Gaspara Stampa
denn genügend gedacht, daß irgendein Mädchen,
dem der Geliebte entging, am gesteigerten Beispiel
dieser Liebenden fühlt: daß ich würde wie sie?
Sollen nicht endlich uns diese ältesten Schmerzen
fruchtbarer werden? Ist es nicht Zeit, daß wir liebend
uns vom Geliebten befrein und es bebend bestehn:
wie der Pfeil die Sehne besteht, um gesammelt im
     Absprung
mehr zu sein als er selbst. Denn Bleiben ist nirgends.

Stimmen, Stimmen. Höre, mein Herz, wie sonst nur
Heilige hörten: daß sie der riesige Ruf
aufhob vom Boden; sie aber knieten,
Unmögliche, weiter und achtetens nicht:
So waren sie hörend. Nicht daß du Gottes ertrügest
die Stimme, bei weitem. Aber das Wehende höre,
die ununterbrochene Nachricht, die aus Stille sich
     bildet.
Es rauscht jetzt von jenen jungen Toten zu dir.
Wo immer du eintratst, redete nicht in Kirchen
zu Rom und Neapel ruhig ihr Schicksal dich an?
Oder es trug eine Inschrift sich erhaben dir auf,
wie neulich die Tafel in Santa Maria Formosa.
Was sie mir wollen? Leise soll ich des Unrechts
Anschein abtun, der ihrer Geister
reine Bewegung manchmal ein wenig behindert.

into herself, as if she hadn't strength to achieve it
a second time. Have you thought enough of Gaspara
    Stampa,*
so that any girl whose lover ran off will feel,
from the heightened example of this loving woman:
"Ah, might I be like her!" Should not these oldest
sorrows finally become more fruitful for us?
Isn't it time that we lovingly free ourselves
from the beloved and stand it, although we tremble,
as the arrow stands the bowstring, tense to be *more*
    than itself?
For abiding is nowhere.

Voices, voices. Listen, my heart, as hitherto only
saints have listened, so that the mighty call
lifted them from the earth; but they kept on kneeling,
these impossible ones, and paid no attention—
so hard they were listening: Not that you could bear
the voice of God—far from it. But hear the wind's
    blowing,
the uninterrupted tidings created from silence,
they sweep toward you now from those who died young.
Whenever you went into a church in Rome or Naples,
did not their fate speak quietly to you?
Or loftily an inscription charged itself upon you,
as recently the tablet in Santa Maria Formosa.
What do they want of me? I must clear away gently
the semblance of injustice that sometimes hinders
a little the pure movement of their spirits.

* A noble Milanese of the sixteenth century who loved and
was deserted. She solaced herself with religion, poetry, and
other lovers.

Freilich ist es seltsam, die Erde nicht mehr zu
    bewohnen,
kaum erlernte Gebräuche nicht mehr zu üben,
Rosen, und andern eigens versprechenden Dingen
nicht die Bedeutung menschlicher Zukunft zu geben;
das, was man war in unendlich ängstlichen Händen,
nicht mehr zu sein, und selbst den eigenen Namen
wegzulassen wie ein zerbrochenes Spielzeug.
Seltsam, die Wünsche nicht weiterzuwünschen.
    Seltsam,
alles, was sich bezog, so lose im Raume
flattern zu sehen. Und das Totsein ist mühsam
und voller Nachholn, daß man allmählich ein wenig
Ewigkeit spürt.—Aber Lebendige machen
alle den Fehler, daß sie zu stark unterscheiden.
Engel (sagt man) wüßten oft nicht, ob sie unter
Lebenden gehn oder Toten. Die ewige Strömung
reißt durch beide Bereiche alle Alter
immer mit sich und übertönt sie in beiden.

Schließlich brauchen sie uns nicht mehr, die Frühe-
    entrückten,
man entwöhnt sich des Irdischen sanft, wie man den
    Brüsten
milde der Mutter entwächst. Aber wir, die so große
Geheimnisse brauchen, denen aus Trauer so oft
seliger Fortschritt entspringt—: *könnten* wir sein
    ohne sie?
Ist die Sage umsonst, daß einst in der Klage um Linos
wagende erste Musik dürre Erstarrung durchdrang,

True, it is strange to live no more on earth,
no longer follow the folkways scarcely learned;
not to give roses and other especially auspicious
things the significance of a human future;
to be no more what one was in infinitely anxious hands,
and to put aside even one's name, like a broken
    plaything.
Strange, to wish wishes no longer. Strange, to see
all that was related fluttering so loosely in space.
And being dead is hard, full of catching-up,
so that finally one feels a little eternity.—
But the living all make the mistake of too sharp
    discrimination.
Often angels (it's said) don't know if they move
among the quick or the dead. The eternal current
hurtles all ages along with it forever
through both realms and drowns their voices in both.

In the end, those taken early no longer need us;
one is gently weaned from earthly things,
even as he tenderly outgrows the breasts of his mother.
But we who need such mighty mysteries,
we for whom blessed advancement so often comes
    from grief:
could we exist without them? Is the legend in vain,
that once in the lamentation for Linos,* the daring
first music pierced the barren numbness, and only

* Linos, like Adonis, was one of the many personifications of
spring. His yearly seasonal death, like that of the departure
of the swallows, came to be celebrated by a lament, a dirge
for the passage of spring. There seems also to have been, in
Rilke's mind, a perhaps intentional connection with the Or-
pheus legend.

daß erst im erschrockenen Raum, dem ein beinah göttlicher Jüngling
  plötzlich für immer enttrat, das Leere in jene
Schwingung geriet, die uns jetzt hinreißt und tröstet
  und hilft.

then in frightened space, which an almost godlike youth
suddenly forsook forever, the void began to feel
that vibration which now enraptures, consoles and
   helps us?

Die Zweite Elegie

Jeder Engel ist schrecklich. Und dennoch, weh mir,
ansing ich euch, fast tödliche Vögel der Seele,
wissend um euch. Wohin sind die Tage Tobiae,
da der Strahlendsten einer stand an der einfachen
    Haustür,
zur Reise ein wenig verkleidet und schon nicht mehr
    furchtbar;
(Jüngling dem Jüngling, wie er neugierig hinaussah).
Träte der Erzengel jetzt, der gefährliche, hinter den
    Sternen
eines Schrittes nur nieder und herwärts: hochauf-
schlagend erschlüg uns das eigene Herz. Wer seid ihr?

Frühe Geglückte, ihr Verwöhnten der Schöpfung,
Höhenzüge, morgenrötliche Grate
aller Erschaffung,—Pollen der blühenden Gottheit,
Gelenke des Lichtes, Gänge, Treppen, Throne,
Räume aus Wesen, Schilde aus Wonne, Tumulte
stürmisch entzückten Gefühls und plötzlich, einzeln,
Spiegel, die die entströmte eigene Schönheit
wiederschöpfen zurück in das eigene Antlitz.

The Second Elegy

Every angel is terrible. And yet, alas,
I welcome you, almost fatal birds of the soul,
knowing about you. Where are the days of Tobias
when one of the most-shining stood by the simple
    house-door,
a little disguised for traveling and no longer frightening
(a youth to the youth when he looked out curiously)?
If the archangel came now, the perilous one,
from back of the stars, but one step lower and
    toward us,
our own high-beating heart would slay us. Who are
    you?

You early successes, spoiled darlings of creation,
mountain ranges, ridges reddened by dawn
of genesis,—pollen of flowering godhead,
articulations of light, corridors, stairways, thrones,
spaces of existence, shields of rapture, tumults
of stormy ecstasy, and suddenly, singly,
mirrors which scoop again their outpoured beauty
back into their own faces.

13

atmen uns aus und dahin; von Holzglut zu Holzglut
geben wir schwächern Geruch. Da sagt uns wohl einer:
ja, du gehst mir ins Blut, dieses Zimmer, der Frühling
füllt sich mit dir ... Was hilfts, er kann uns nicht
    halten,
wir schwinden in ihm und um ihn. Und jene, die
    schön sind,
o wer hält sie zurück? Unaufhörlich steht Anschein
auf in ihrem Gesicht und geht fort. Wie Tau von
    dem Frühgras
hebt sich das Unsre von uns, wie die Hitze von einem
heißen Gericht. O Lächeln, wohin? O Aufschaun:
neue, warme, entgehende Welle des Herzens—;
weh mir: wir *sinds* doch. Schmeckt denn der Weltraum,
in den wir uns lösen, nach uns? Fangen die Engel
wirklich nur Ihriges auf, ihnen Entströmtes,
oder ist manchmal, wie aus Versehen, ein wenig
unseres Wesens dabei? Sind wir in ihre
Züge soviel nur gemischt wie das Vage in die Gesichter
schwangerer Frauen? Sie merken es nicht in dem
    Wirbel
ihrer Rückkehr zu sich. (Wie sollten sie's merken.)

Liebende könnten, verstünden sie's, in der Nachtluft
wunderlich reden. Denn es scheint, daß uns alles
verheimlicht. Siehe, die Bäume *sind*; die Häuser,
die wir bewohnen, bestehn noch. Wir nur
ziehen allem vorbei wie ein luftiger Austausch.
Und alles ist einig, uns zu verschweigen, halb als
Schande vielleicht und halb als unsägliche Hoffnung.

Liebende, euch, ihr ineinander Genügten,
frag ich nach uns. Ihr greift euch. Habt ihr Beweise?

For when we feel,
we evaporate. Ah, we breathe ourselves out and afar;
from ember to ember, we give off a fainter smell.
Then perhaps someone says: "Yes, you've got into
    my blood;
this room, the spring is filling itself with you"...
No use. He cannot hold us. We disappear
in and around him. And those who are lovely, oh,
who holds them back? Unceasingly appearance
mounts into their faces and goes away.
Like dew from the morning grass, that which is ours
rises from us, like heat from a hot dish.
O smile, whereto? O upward gaze, new, warm,
escaping wave of the heart—alas, we *are* that.
Does the cosmic space in which we dissolve taste of us?
Do the angels really seize nothing but what is theirs,
what has streamed from them, or sometimes, as
    if by mistake,
is a bit of our being with it? Are we mixed in their
    features
like the vagueness on the faces of pregnant women?
They're not aware of it in the whirl of returning
into themselves? (How should they notice it?)

Lovers, if they knew it, could speak strangely
in the night air. For it seems that everything
is keeping us a secret. Look: the trees *are*;
the houses we live in still stand. Only we go
past everything like a bartering of the breeze.
And everything conspires to silence us,
half as shame, perhaps, and half as unspeakable hope.

You lovers, self-sufficient, I ask you
about us. You hold each other. Have you proof?

The Second Elegy 15

Seht, mir geschiehts, daß meine Hände einander
inne werden oder daß mein gebrauchtes
Gesicht in ihnen sich schont. Das gibt mir ein wenig
Empfindung. Doch wer wagte darum schon zu *sein*?
Ihr aber, die ihr im Entzücken des andern
zunehmt, bis er euch überwältigt
anfleht: nicht *mehr*—; die ihr unter den Händen
euch reichlicher werdet wie Traubenjahre;
die ihr manchmal vergeht, nur weil der andre
ganz überhandnimmt: euch frag ich nach uns. Ich
    weiß,
ihr berührt euch so selig, weil die Liebkosung verhält,
weil die Stelle nicht schwindet, die ihr, Zärtliche,
zudeckt; weil ihr darunter das reine
Dauern verspürt. So versprecht ihr euch Ewigkeit fast
von der Umarmung. Und doch, wenn ihr der ersten
Blicke Schrecken besteht und die Sehnsucht am Fenster
und den ersten gemeinsamen Gang, *ein* Mal durch
    den Garten:
Liebende, *seid* ihrs dann noch? Wenn ihr einer dem
    andern
euch an den Mund hebt und ansetzt—: Getränk
    an Getränk:
o wie entgeht dann der Trinkende seltsam der
    Handlung.

Erstaunte euch nicht auf attischen Stelen die Vorsicht
menschlicher Geste? war nicht Liebe und Abschied
so leicht auf die Schultern gelegt, als wär es aus anderm
Stoffe gemacht als bei uns? Gedenkt euch der Hände,
wie sie drucklos beruhen, obwohl in den Torsen die
    Kraft steht.
Diese Beherrschten wußten damit: so weit sind wirs,

Look, it happens sometimes that my hands
become aware of each other or that my worn face
saves itself in them. That gives me a little sensation.
Yet who, for that, would dare *exist*?
But you who increase yourselves in each other's rapture
until, overcome, he begs of you: "No more."—
You, under each other's hands growing more abundant,
like grapes in a vintage year; you who often droop,
    merely
because the other completely takes over:
I ask you about us. I know you touch each other
so blissfully because the caress holds back,
because the place you tender ones cover does not
    disappear;
because you feel pure permanence underneath.
So you promise yourself almost eternity
from the embrace. And yet, if you withstand
the shock of the first glances, the yearning by windows,
and the first walk together, *once*, in the garden:
lovers, *are* you still that? When you give yourselves,
each to the other's mouth and join—drink for
    drink—oh,
how strangely the drinker evades his part of the act.

Were you not astonished by the caution
of human gestures on the Attic stelæ?
Were not love and parting so lightly laid
on the shoulders, as if they were made of other stuff
than with us? remember how the hands touch
    without pressing,
although there is strength in the torsos. These
    self-controlled ones
knew herewith: We are come thus far. Thus much
    is ours:

dieses ist unser, uns *so* zu berühren; stärker
stemmen die Götter uns an. Doch dies ist Sache der
  Götter.

Fänden auch wir ein reines, verhaltenes, schmales
Menschliches, einen unseren Streifen Fruchtlands
zwischen Strom und Gestein. Denn das eigene Herz
  übersteigt uns
noch immer wie jene. Und wir können ihm nicht mehr
nachschaun in Bilder, die es besänftigen, noch in
göttliche Körper, in denen es größer sich mäßigt.

to touch each other *so*. The gods press on us
more strongly, but that's the concern of the gods.

Could we but find a pure, reserved, narrow
humanity: a strip of fertile fruit-land of our own,
between the rock and the river! For our heart
surmounts us always, like theirs. And we can no longer
gaze after it into images
that soothe it down, or into godlike bodies
wherein it tempers itself more loftily.

Die Dritte Elegie

Eines ist, die Geliebte zu singen. Ein anderes, wehe,
jenen verborgenen schuldigen Fluß-Gott des Bluts.
Den sie von weitem erkennt, ihren Jüngling, was
    weiß er
selbst von dem Herren der Lust, der aus dem
    Einsamen oft,
ehe das Mädchen noch linderte, oft auch als wäre sie
    nicht,
ach, von welchem Unkenntlichen triefend, das
    Gotthaupt
aufhob, aufrufend die Nacht zu unendlichem Aufruhr.
O des Blutes Neptun, o sein furchtbarer Dreizack.
O der dunkele Wind seiner Brust aus gewundener
    Muschel.
Horch, wie die Nacht sich muldet und höhlt. Ihr
    Sterne,
stammt nicht von euch des Liebenden Lust zu dem
    Antlitz
seiner Geliebten? Hat er die innige Einsicht
in ihr reines Gesicht nicht aus dem reinen Gestirn?

The Third Elegy

It is one thing to sing the beloved. Another, alas,
to sing that hidden guilty river-god of the blood.
He whom she knows from afar, her young lover, what
does he know of the lord of desire, who from his
    loneliness
often (before the girl eased him, often as if
she did not exist) raised his godhead, dripping with
    what
Unknowable, calling forth the night to infinite tumult?
Oh, Neptune of the blood, oh, his dreadful trident!
Oh, the dark wind of his breast from the spiral conch!
Listen, how night troughs out and hollows itself.
You stars, is it not from you that the lover's desire
for the dear face springs? Has he not his tender insight
into her pure face from the pure constellations?

Du nicht hast ihm, wehe, nicht seine Mutter
hat ihm die Bogen der Braun so zur Erwartung
    gespannt.
Nicht an dir, ihn fühlendes Mädchen, an dir nicht
bog seine Lippe sich zum fruchtbarern Ausdruck.
Meinst du wirklich, ihn hätte dein leichter Auftritt
also erschüttert, du, die wandelt wie Frühwind?
Zwar du erschrakst ihm das Herz; doch ältere Schrecken
stürzten in ihn bei dem berührenden Anstoß.
Ruf ihn . . . du rufst ihn nicht ganz aus dunkelem
    Umgang.
Freilich, er *will*, er entspringt; erleichtert gewöhnt er
sich in dein heimliches Herz und nimmt und beginnt
    sich.
Aber begann er sich je?
Mutter, *du* machtest ihn klein, du warsts, die ihn
    anfing;
dir war er neu, du beugtest über die neuen
Augen die freundliche Welt und wehrtest der fremden.
Wo, ach, hin sind die Jahre, da du ihm einfach
mit der schlanken Gestalt wallendes Chaos vertratst?
Vieles verbargst du ihm so; das nächtlich verdächtige
    Zimmer
machtest du harmlos, aus deinem Herzen voll Zuflucht
mischtest du menschlichern Raum seinem Nacht-
    Raum hinzu.
Nicht in die Finsternis, nein, in dein näheres Dasein
hast du das Nachtlicht gestellt, und es schien wie aus
    Freundschaft.
Nirgends ein Knistern, das du nicht lächelnd erklärtest,
so als wüßtest du längst, *wann* sich die Diele
    benimmt . . .
Und er horchte und linderte sich. So vieles vermochte
zärtlich dein Aufstehn; hinter den Schrank trat

You did not, alas, his mother did not bend
the bows of his brows to this suspense. Not on you,
girl who feel him, not on you did his mouth
curve itself to this more fruitful expression.
Do you really imagine that your light steps
so shook him, you who move like the wind of dawn?
Surely, you frightened his heart; but older terrors
plunged into him at the shock of contact. Call him . . .
you cannot call him quite from that dark concourse.
Really, he *wills* to, he does escape; relieved,
he grows at home in your inmost heart and takes
and begins himself there. But did he begin himself ever?
Mother, *you* made him small, it was you undertook
    him;
he was new to you, you curved above his young eyes
the friendly world and shut the strange one out.
Ah, where have the years gone when your slender body
simply debarred the surging chaos from him?
Much you hid from him thus; you made harmless
    the room
suspect at night; from your heart full of refuge
you mingled human space with the space of his night.
Not in the darkness, no, in your closer presence
you placed the night-light, and it shone as from
    friendship.
Never a creak you didn't explain with a smile,
as if you had long known *when* the floor would
    act up . . .
and he listened to you and calmed down. This much
    your tender
getting-up achieved; and, tall in his mantle, his fate
withdrew behind the wardrobe, and his troubled

hoch im Mantel sein Schicksal, und in die Falten des
   Vorhangs
paßte, die leicht sich verschob, seine unruhige Zukunft.

Und er selbst, wie er lag, der Erleichterte, unter
schläfernden Lidern deiner leichten Gestaltung
Süße lösend in den gekosteten Vorschlaf—:
schien ein Gehüteter . . . Aber *innen:* wer wehrte,
hinderte innen in ihm die Fluten der Herkunft?
Ach, da *war* keine Vorsicht im Schlafenden; schlafend,
aber träumend, aber in Fiebern: wie er sich ein-ließ.
Er, der Neue, Scheuende, wie er verstrickt war,
mit des innern Geschehns weiterschlagenden Ranken
schon zu Mustern verschlungen, zu würgendem
   Wachstum, zu tierhaft
jagenden Formen. Wie er sich hingab—. Liebte.
Liebte sein Inneres, seines Inneren Wildnis,
diesen Urwald in ihm, auf dessen stummem
   Gestürztsein
lichtgrün sein Herz stand. Liebte. Verließ es, ging die
eigenen Wurzeln hinaus in gewaltigen Ursprung,
wo seine kleine Geburt schon überlebt war. Liebend
stieg er hinab in das ältere Blut, in die Schluchten,
wo das Furchtbare lag, noch satt von den Vätern.
   Und jedes
Schreckliche kannte ihn, blinzelte, war wie verständigt.
Ja, das Entsetzliche lächelte . . . Selten
hast du so zärtlich gelächelt, Mutter. Wie sollte
er es nicht lieben, da es ihm lächelte. *Vor* dir
hat ers geliebt, denn, da du ihn trugst schon,
war es im Wasser gelöst, das den Keimenden leicht
   macht.

Siehe, wir lieben nicht, wie die Blumen, aus einem

future, lightly shifting, adapted itself
among the folds of the curtain.

And he himself, as he lay there, comforted,
under the drowsy lids of your light molding,
dissolving its sweetness in the first sip of sleep,
seemed one well-guarded . . . but *within*, who fended,
hindered within him the flood-tides of origin?
Ah, there *was* no caution in that sleeper; sleeping,
but dreaming, but in fever, how he yielded himself.
He, the new, the shy one, how he got entangled
in the farther-grasping tendrils of inner action
coming to pass, already interwoven as patterns,
as strangling growths, as shapes of beasts of prey.
How he gave himself to it! Loved. Loved his innerness,
his wilderness within, this primeval forest inside him,
on whose silent debris of collapse light-green his
    heart stood.
Loved. Left it, went from his own roots into the
    powerful
sources where his little birth was already
outlived. Lovingly he went down into the older
blood, the gorges where terror lay, still glutted
with the forefathers. And every horror knew him,
winked and knew what was doing. Yes,
the monstrous smiled . . . seldom,
mother, have you smiled so tenderly. How
should he not love it, since it smiled for him?
Before you he loved it; for even while you carried him,
it was dissolved in the water that lightens the embryo.

Remember, we don't love like the flowers, from a single

einzigen Jahr; uns steigt, wo wir lieben,
unvordenklicher Saft in die Arme. O Mädchen,
dies: daß wir liebten *in* uns, nicht Eines, ein
    Künftiges, sondern
das zahllos Brauende; nicht ein einzelnes Kind,
sondern die Väter, die wie Trümmer Gebirgs
uns im Grunde beruhn; sondern das trockene Flußbett
einstiger Mütter—; sondern die ganze
lautlose Landschaft unter dem wolkigen oder
reinen Verhängnis —: *dies* kam dir, Mädchen, zuvor.

Und du selber, was weißt du—, du locktest
Vorzeit empor in dem Liebenden. Welche Gefühle
wühlten herauf aus entwandelten Wesen. Welche
Frauen haßten dich da. Was für finstere Männer
regtest du auf im Geäder des Jünglings? Tote
Kinder wollten zu dir . . . O leise, leise,
tu ein liebes vor ihm, ein verläßliches Tagwerk,—
    führ ihn
nah an den Garten heran, gib ihm der Nächte
Übergewicht . . .
       Verhalt ihn . . .

year only; when we love, arises in our arms
the sap from immemorial ages. O young girl,
this: that we loved *within* us, not one, one coming,
but the countless ones teeming; not a single child,
but the fathers who rest in our depths, like the ruins
      of mountains;
but the dry riverbed of foremothers; but the whole
silent landscape under the clear or
cloudy destiny: all *this* forestalled you, young woman.

And you yourself, what do you know? You called forth
past ages in your lover. What feelings stormed up
from bygone beings! What women hated you there.
What scowling men didn't you stir up in the veins
      of the stripling!
Dead children strained toward you . . . oh, gently,
      gently,
do for his sake a trustworthy day's work.
Lead him near the garden. Give him
the preponderance of the nights . . .
                              Restrain him . . .

Die Vierte Elegie

O Bäume Lebens, o wann winterlich?
Wir sind nicht einig. Sind nicht wie die Zug-
vögel verständigt. Überholt und spät,
so drängen wir uns plötzlich Winden auf
und fallen ein auf teilnahmslosen Teich.
Blühn und verdorrn ist uns zugleich bewußt.
Und irgendwo gehn Löwen noch und wissen,
solang sie herrlich sind, von keiner Ohnmacht.

Uns aber, wo wir eines meinen ganz,
ist schon des andern Aufwand fühlbar. Feindschaft
ist uns das Nächste. Treten Liebende
nicht immerfort an Ränder, eins im andern,
die sich versprachen Weite, Jagd und Heimat.
Da wird für eines Augenblickes Zeichnung
ein Grund von Gegenteil bereitet, mühsam,
daß wir sie sähen; denn man ist sehr deutlich
mit uns. Wir kennen den Kontur
des Fühlens nicht, nur was ihn formt von außen.
Wer saß nicht bang vor seines Herzens Vorhang?

The Fourth Elegy

O Trees of life, oh, when winterly?
We're not in accord. Are not of one mind
like birds of passage. Overtaken and belated,
we force ourselves abruptly on the winds
and fall into an indifferent pond. We understand
blooming and withering alike. And somewhere
lions are still wandering and do not know,
in their lordliness, of any weakness.

But we, when we purpose one thing wholly, already
feel the outlay of the other. Enmity
is closest to us. Do not lovers always
come to the brink, one in the other, they
who promised themselves space, the chase, and
    a homeland?
There for an eyewink's sketch a foundation
for the opposite's laboriously got ready,
so we can see it; for it's very plain to us
that we don't know the contour of the feelings,
    but only
what molds it from without. Who has not sat,
anxious, before the curtain of his heart?

Der schlug sich auf: die Szenerie war Abschied.
Leicht zu verstehen. Der bekannte Garten,
und schwankte leise: dann erst kam der Tänzer.
Nicht *der*. Genug. Und wenn er auch so leicht tut,
er ist verkleidet, und er wird ein Bürger
und geht durch seine Küche in die Wohnung.
Ich will nicht diese halbgefüllten Masken,
lieber die Puppe. Die ist voll. Ich will
den Balg aushalten und den Draht und ihr
Gesicht aus Aussehn. Hier. Ich bin davor.
Wenn auch die Lampen ausgehn, wenn mir auch
gesagt wird: Nichts mehr—, wenn auch von der Bühne
das Leere herkommt mit dem grauen Luftzug,
wenn auch von meinen stillen Vorfahrn keiner
mehr mit mir dasitzt, keine Frau, sogar
der Knabe nicht mehr mit dem braunen Schielaug:
Ich bleibe dennoch. Es gibt immer Zuschaun.

Hab ich nicht recht? Du, der um mich so bitter
das Leben schmeckte, meines kostend, Vater,
den ersten trüben Aufguß meines Müssens,
da ich heranwuchs, immer wieder kostend
und, mit dem Nachgeschmack so fremder Zukunft
beschäftigt, prüftest mein beschlagnes Aufschaun, —
der du, mein Vater, seit du tot bist, oft
in meiner Hoffnung, innen in mir, Angst hast,
und Gleichmut, wie ihn Tote haben, Reiche
von Gleichmut, aufgibst für mein bißchen Schicksal,
hab ich nicht recht? Und ihr, hab ich nicht recht,
die ihr mich liebtet für den kleinen Anfang
Liebe zu euch, von dem ich immer abkam,
weil mir der Raum in eurem Angesicht,
da ich ihn liebte, überging in Weltraum,
in dem ihr nicht mehr wart ... Wenn mir zumut ist,

Then it went up, and the stage-setting was Parting.
Simple to understand. The familiar garden,
and it swayed gently. Only then came the dancer.
Not *he*. Enough. But however nimbly he acts,
he's in disguise and turns out to be a townsman
who goes into his house by way of the kitchen.
I don't want these half-filled masks, no, rather the doll.
It's full. I'll put up with the skin and the wires
and the face that's only appearance. I'm out here
    in front.
Even if the footlights go out and I'm told: That's all—
if emptiness from the stage blows in gray drafts,
if none of my silent forefathers sits beside me,
no woman, not even the boy with brown squint-eyes:
I'll stay, in spite of it. One can always look on.

Am I not right, father? You to whom life
tasted so bitter for my sake, as you tried mine:
the first muddy infusions of my necessity;
as I grew up, you kept on tasting, engrossed
by the after-flavor of so strange a future,
and you tried out my misted upward gaze.
You, my father, who often since you are dead
have worried about me inside my hope, renouncing
serenity, such as the dead possess;
realms of serenity, for my crumb of fate.
Isn't that right? And you—am I not right?—
who loved me for my little beginning of love
for you, from which I always veered, because
of the distance in your face (even while I loved it)
passed into cosmic space, where you weren't any
    more . . .

zu warten vor der Puppenbühne, nein,
so völlig hinzuschaun, daß, um mein Schauen
am Ende aufzuwiegen, dort als Spieler
ein Engel hinmuß, der die Bälge hochreißt.
Engel und Puppe: dann ist endlich Schauspiel.
Dann kommt zusammen, was wir immerfort
entzwein, indem wir da sind. Dann entsteht
aus unsern Jahreszeiten erst der Umkreis
des ganzen Wandelns. Über uns hinüber
spielt dann der Engel. Sieh, die Sterbenden,
sollten sie nicht vermuten, wie voll Vorwand
das alles ist, was wir hier leisten. Alles
ist nicht es selbst. O Stunden in der Kindheit,
da hinter den Figuren mehr als nur
Vergangnes war und vor uns nicht die Zukunft.
Wir wuchsen freilich, und wir drängten manchmal,
bald groß zu werden, denen halb zulieb,
die andres nicht mehr hatten als das Großsein.
Und waren doch in unserem Alleingehn
mit Dauerndem vergnügt und standen da
im Zwischenraume zwischen Welt und Spielzeug,
an einer Stelle, die seit Anbeginn
gegründet war für einen reinen Vorgang.

Wer zeigt ein Kind, so wie es steht? Wer stellt
es ins Gestirn und gibt das Maß des Abstands
ihm in die Hand? Wer macht den Kindertod
aus grauem Brot, das hart wird, —oder läßt
ihn drin im runden Mund so wie den Gröps
von einem schönen Apfel? ... Mörder sind
leicht einzusehen. Aber dies: den Tod,
den ganzen Tod, noch *vor* dem Leben so
sanft zu enthalten und nicht bös zu sein,
ist unbeschreiblich.

When I'm in the humor to watch the marionettes, no,
but to gaze so hard that at last, to balance my gazing,
an angel must come as a player to quicken the puppet.
Angel and marionette: then at last there's a show.
Then is rejoined what we by our being here
have always sundered. Then first from our seasons arises
the circle of full transformation. Above and beyond us
the angel is playing. Look: must not the dying
guess how full of subterfuge is all we achieve here?
Nothing is anything. Oh, hours of childhood,
when behind the symbols was more than merely
    the past,
and before us was not the future. Sure, we were
    growing,
and often we strove to grow up sooner, half
for the sake of those who had nothing but being
    grown-up.
Yet we were content in our going alone
with things that last, and we stood there in the breach
between the world and the plaything, on a place
founded from the first for a pure event.

Who shows a child just as he is? Who sets him
in a constellation and puts the measuring-stick
of distance in his hands? Who makes the child's death
out of gray bread that grows hard, or leaves it there
in the round mouth, like the core of a fine apple? . . .
Murderers are easily seen through. But this:
to accept death, even *before* life, so gently,
the whole of death, and not to be angry,
is past description.

Die Fünfte Elegie

Frau Hertha Koenig zugeeignet

Wer aber *sind* sie, sag mir, die Fahrenden, diese ein
    wenig
Flüchtigern noch als wir selbst, die dringend von
    früh an
wringt ein wem—wem zuliebe
niemals zufriedener Wille? Sondern er wringt sie,
biegt sie, schlingt sie und schwingt sie,
wirft sie und fängt sie zurück; wie aus geölter,
glatterer Luft kommen sie nieder
auf dem verzehrten, von ihrem ewigen
Aufsprung dünneren Teppich, diesem verlorenen
Teppich im Weltall.
Aufgelegt wie ein Pflaster, als hätte der Vorstadt-
Himmel der Erde dort wehegetan.
                    Und kaum dort,
aufrecht, da und gezeigt: des Dastehns
großer Anfangsbuchstab..., schon auch, die stärksten
Männer, rollt sie wieder, zum Scherz, der immer

The Fifth Elegy

But tell me, who *are* these vagrants, these even a little
more transitory than we, these from the start
violently wrung (and for whose sake?)
by a never-appeasable will? But it wrings them,
bends them, slings them and swings them,
throws them and catches them; as if from an oily,
more slippery air they come down
on the carpet worn thinner by their eternal leaping,
this carpet lost in the universe.
Stuck there like a plaster, as if the sky
of the suburb had hurt the earth.

                       And scarcely there,
erect, here and on show: the great initial letter
of Durance . . . for the ever-advancing grip*
rolls even the strongest men once more, just for fun,

* The D of Dastehen, literally, "Standing-thereness," must
be preserved because the acrobats in Picasso's picture, *Les
Saltimbanques*, are grouped in this form, and the elegy shaped
itself about this painting.

kommende Griff, wie August der Starke bei Tisch
einen zinnenen Teller.

Ach und um diese
Mitte, die Rose des Zuschauns:
blüht und entblättert. Um diesen
Stampfer, den Stempel, den von dem eignen
blühenden Staub getroffnen, zur Scheinfrucht
wieder der Unlust befruchteten, ihrer
niemals bewußten,—glänzend mit dünnster
Oberfläche leicht scheinlächelnden Unlust.

Da, der welke, faltige Stemmer,
der alte, der nur noch trommelt,
eingegangen in seiner gewaltigen Haut, als hätte sie
    früher
zwei Männer enthalten, und einer
läge nun schon auf dem Kirchhof, und er überlebte
    den andern,
taub und manchmal ein wenig
wirr, in der verwitweten Haut.

Aber der junge, der Mann, als wär er der Sohn eines
    Nackens
und einer Nonne: prall und strammig erfüllt
mit Muskeln und Einfalt.

O ihr,
die ein Leid, das noch klein war,
einst als Spielzeug bekam, in einer seiner
langen Genesungen . . .

Du, der mit dem Aufschlag,
wie nur Früchte ihn kennen, unreif

36 *Die Fünfte Elegie*

as King Augustus the Strong toyed at table*
with a pewter platter.

Ah, and around this center,
the rose of gazing
blooms and loses its petals. Around this pestle,
the pistil, touched by its own fertile pollen,
impregnated again to become
the illusory fruit of disgust, of their never-conscious,
shining with superficial,
light, sham-smiling disgust.

There, the shriveled, wrinkled weight-lifter,
the old man who only drums now,
shrunken into his powerful skin, as if
it had once held *two* men, and the other
already lay in the churchyard, and this one outlived him,
deaf and often a little confused
in the widowed skin.

But the young one, the man, as if he were the son
of a neck and a nun: tense and tightly packed
with muscles and dumbness.

O you
whom a pain that was still small
got for a plaything once, in one of its
long spells of convalescence . . .

You, who with the impact,
that only unripened fruits know, daily

* This king of Saxony, among other feats of strength, sired
three hundred children.

täglich hundert Mal abfällt vom Baum der gemeinsam
erbauten Bewegung, (der, rascher als Wasser, in wenig
Minuten Lenz, Sommer und Herbst hat) —
abfällt und anprallt ans Grab:
manchmal, in halber Pause, will dir ein liebes
Antlitz entstehn hinüber zu deiner selten
zärtlichen Mutter; doch an deinen Körper verliert sich,
der es flächig verbraucht, das schüchtern
kaum versuchte Gesicht . . . Und wieder
klatscht der Mann in die Hand zu dem Ansprung,
 und eh dir
jemals ein Schmerz deutlicher wird in der Nähe des
 immer
trabenden Herzens, kommt das Brennen der Fußsohln
ihm, seinem Ursprung, zuvor mit ein paar dir
rasch in die Augen gejagten leiblichen Tränen.
Und dennoch, blindlings,
das Lächeln . . .

Engel! o nimms, pflücks, das kleinblütige Heilkraut.
Schaff eine Vase, verwahrs! Stells unter jene, uns
 noch nicht
offenen Freuden; in lieblicher Urne
rühms mit blumiger, schwungiger Aufschrift:
                              „Subrisio Saltat."

Du dann, Liebliche,
du, von den reizendsten Freuden
stumm Übersprungne. Vielleicht sind
deine Fransen glücklich für dich—,
oder über den jungen
prallen Brüsten die grüne metallene Seide
fühlt sich unendlich verwöhnt und entbehrt nichts.
Du, auf alle des Gleichgewichts schwankende Wagen

a hundred times fall from the tree of the built-up
stunt of the group (that, swifter than water, has spring,
summer and autumn in a few instants)
fall and bounce on the grave:
often, in a half-pause, a loving look wants
to rise in your face toward your rarely tender mother,
but loses itself on your body whose surface consumes
the timid scarcely begun glance . . . and once more
the man claps his hands for the leap, and before
a pain is more sharply felt near your ever-pounding
heart, the burning of your soles is ahead
of its cause, with a few tears from your body driven
quickly into your eyes. And nonetheless, blindly,
the smile . . .

Oh, take it, angel! gather this small-flowered simple.
Create a vase, preserve it. Put it among those joys
not yet open to us. On the delicate urn
laud it with flowery flowing inscription:
                    "Subrisio Saltat." *

Then you, darling,
mutely leaped over
by the most exciting joys. Maybe your fringes
are happy for you,—or over the firm young breasts
the green metallic silk
feels itself endlessly pampered and lacks nothing.
You, a market-fruit of resignation

* "Saltat" is an abbreviation of *saltatoris*. In English this
would read: "Acrobat's Smile."

immerfort anders
hingelegte Marktfrucht des Gleichmuts,
öffentlich unter den Schultern.

Wo, o *wo* ist der Ort,—ich trag ihn im Herzen —,
wo sie noch lange nicht *konnten*, noch von einander
abfieln, wie sich bespringende, nicht recht
paarige Tiere;—
wo die Gewichte noch schwer sind;
wo noch von ihren vergeblich
wirbelnden Stäben die Teller
torkeln ...

Und plötzlich in diesem mühsamen Nirgends, plötzlich
die unsägliche Stelle, wo sich das reine Zuwenig
unbegreiflich verwandelt—, umspringt
in jenes leere Zuviel.
Wo die vielstellige Rechnung
zahlenlos aufgeht.

Plätze, o Platz in Paris, unendlicher Schauplatz,
wo die Modistin, *Madame Lamort*,
die ruhlosen Wege der Erde, endlose Bänder,
schlingt und windet und neue aus ihnen
Schleifen erfindet, Rüschen, Blumen, Kokarden,
    künstliche Früchte—, alle
unwahr gefärbt,—für die billigen
Winterhüte des Schicksals.

.   .   .   .

Engel: es wäre ein Platz, den wir nicht wissen, und
    dorten,
auf unsäglichem Teppich, zeigten die Liebenden,
    die's hier

always differently displayed
on the wavering scale-pans of equipoise,
public among the shoulders.

Where, oh, where is the place—I bear it in my heart—
where for a long time they *could* not, but fell from
   each other
like rutting animals, not rightly mated;
where the dumbbells are still heavy,
where still from the vainly twirled wands
the platters spin away,
wobbling? . . .

And suddenly in this tedious Nowhere, suddenly
the ineffable place where pure dearth
is inconceivably transmuted—changes
into this empty surfeit.
Where the reckoning of many columns
totals to zero.

Squares, O square of Paris, eternal showplace,
where the milliner, Madame Lamort,
twines and winds the restless roads of the earth,
endless ribbons, invents with them new bows,
ruches, flowers, cockades, artificial fruits—
all falsely colored—for the bargain
winter hats of fate.

. . . .

Angel, if there were a place we don't know, and there
on some ineffable carpet, the lovers, who never

bis zum Können nie bringen, ihre kühnen
hohen Figuren des Herzschwungs,
ihre Türme aus Lust, ihre
längst, wo Boden nie war, nur aneinander
lehnenden Leitern, bebend,—und *könntens,*
vor den Zuschauern rings, unzähligen lautlosen Toten:
Würfen die dann ihre letzten, immer ersparten,
immer verborgenen, die wir nicht kennen, ewig
gültigen Münzen des Glücks vor das endlich
wahrhaft lächelnde Paar auf gestilltem
Teppich?

could bring off their feats here, could show
their bold lofty figures of heart-swings,
their towers of ecstasy, their pyramids
that long since, where there was no standing-ground,
were tremblingly propped together—*could* succeed
before the spectators around them, the innumerable
    silent dead:
would not these then throw their last, ever-hoarded,
ever-hidden, unknown to us, eternally
valid coins of happiness
before that pair with the finally genuine smile
on the assuaged carpet?

Die Sechste Elegie

Feigenbaum, seit wie lange schon ists mir bedeutend,
wie du die Blüte beinah ganz überschlägst
und hinein in die zeitig entschlossene Frucht,
ungerühmt, drängst dein reines Geheimnis.
Wie der Fontäne Rohr treibt dein gebognes Gezweig
abwärts den Saft und hinan: und es springt aus dem
    Schlaf,
fast nicht erwachend, ins Glück seiner süßesten
    Leistung.
Sieh: wie der Gott in den Schwan.
                    . . . Wir aber verweilen,
ach, uns rühmt es zu blühn, und ins verspätete Innre
unserer endlichen Frucht gehn wir verraten hinein.
Wenigen steigt so stark der Andrang des Handelns,
daß sie schon anstehn und glühn in der Fülle des
    Herzens,
wenn die Verführung zum Blühn wie gelinderte
    Nachtluft
ihnen die Jugend des Munds, ihnen die Lider berührt:
Helden vielleicht und den frühe Hinüberbestimmten,

The Sixth Elegy

Fig tree, for ever so long it's meant much to me
how you almost completely skip over the blooming
and into the timely determined fruit, unpraised,
press your pure secret. Like the pipe of a fountain,
your bent branches force the sap downward and up,
and scarcely awakened it leaps from sleep
into the happiness of sweetest achievement.
See! like the god in the swan.

                         ... But we linger,
ah, our fame is in flowering; revealed already,
we enter the retarded quintessence of our ultimate fruit.
In few does the surging of action mount so strongly,
that they're standing by already, with full glowing
    hearts,
when the temptation to bloom like tempered night-air
touches the youth of their mouths, touches their eyelids:
only in heroes perhaps and those chosen for early
    departure,

denen der gärtnernde Tod anders die Adern verbiegt.
Diese stürzen dahin: dem eigenen Lächeln
sind sie voran, wie das Rossegespann in den milden
muldigen Bildern von Karnak dem siegenden König.

Wunderlich nah ist der Held doch den jugendlich
    Toten. Dauern
ficht ihn nicht an. Sein Aufgang ist Dasein; beständig
nimmt er sich fort und tritt ins veränderte Sternbild
seiner steten Gefahr. Dort fänden ihn wenige. Aber,
das uns finster verschweigt, das plötzlich begeisterte
    Schicksal
singt ihn hinein in den Sturm seiner aufrauschenden
    Welt.
Hör ich doch keinen wie *ihn*. Auf einmal durchgeht
    mich
mit der strömenden Luft sein verdunkelter Ton.

Dann, wie verbärg ich mich gern vor der Sehnsucht:
    O wär ich,
wär ich ein Knabe und dürft es noch werden und säße
in die künftigen Arme gestützt und läse von Simson,
wie seine Mutter erst nichts und dann alles gebar.

War er nicht Held schon in dir, o Mutter, begann nicht
dort schon, in dir, seine herrische Auswahl?
Tausende brauten im Schooß und wollten *er* sein,
aber sieh: er ergriff und ließ aus, wählte und konnte.
Und wenn er Säulen zerstieß, so wars, da er ausbrach
aus der Welt deines Leibs in die engere Welt, wo er
    weiter
wählte und konnte. O Mütter der Helden,
o Ursprung reißender Ströme! Ihr Schluchten, in die
    sich

in whom the gardener Death has otherwise twisted
   the veins.
These hurtle onward, ahead of their smile, like the span
of noble stallions before the conquering king
on the gently molded bas-reliefs at Karnak.

Strangely near is the hero to those who died young.
Permanence does not tempt him. His rise is Being.
Steadfastly he goes onward and enters the changed
   constellation
of his perpetual danger. Few could find him there.
But fate, that darkly conceals us, inspired of a sudden,
sings him into the tempest of his blustering world.
I hear no one else like him. All at once his
obscured shout on the streaming air cuts through me.

Then how I'd like to hide myself from this hankering:
Oh, if I were, if I were a boy and could still
become it, and sat, propped on the future arms,
and read about Samson, how his mother
at first bore nothing and afterward bore all!

Wasn't he hero already within you, O mother,
did not his imperious choice already begin there
   within you?
Thousands teemed in the womb and wished to be *him*.
But look: he seized and refused, he chose and could
   do it.
And when he threw down the pillars, it was when
he burst from the world of your body into the straiter
world, where he chose further and could do it.
O mothers of heroes, O wellsprings of raging torrents!
You gorges, in which, high on the rim of the heart,

hoch von dem Herzrand, klagend,
schon die Mädchen gestürzt, künftig die Opfer dem
   Sohn.
Denn hinstürmte der Held durch Aufenthalte der
   Liebe,
jeder hob ihn hinaus, jeder ihn meinende Herzschlag,
abgewendet schon, stand er am Ende der Lächeln,
   anders.

lamenting, the virgins long since flung themselves,
sacrifices for the son, in the future.
For the hero went storming through the lodgings
    of love,
and every well-meaning heart-throb
thrust him upward and on;
already turning, he stood at the end of smiles, another.

Die Siebente Elegie

Werbung nicht mehr, nicht Werbung, entwachsene
  Stimme,
sei deines Schreies Natur; zwar schrieest du rein wie
  der Vogel,
wenn ihn die Jahreszeit aufhebt, die steigende, beinah
  vergessend,
daß er ein kümmerndes Tier und nicht nur ein
  einzelnes Herz sei,
das sie ins Heitere wirft, in die innigen Himmel.
  Wie er, so
würbest du wohl, nicht minder—, daß, noch
  unsichtbar,
dich die Freundin erführ, die stille, in der eine
  Antwort
langsam erwacht und über dem Hören sich anwärmt,—
deinem erkühnten Gefühl die erglühte Gefühlin.

O und der Frühling begriffe—, da ist keine Stelle,
die nicht trüge den Ton Verkündigung. Erst jenen
  kleinen

The Seventh Elegy

Wooing no more, not wooing, but the voice sprung
    from it,
be the purport of your cry; though your call were
    pure as a bird's,
when the upheaving season lifts him, almost forgetting
that he's a troubled thing, not merely a single heart
tossed by spring to the cheerful tender sky.
Like him, no less, you want to be after some yet unseen
mate who'll be aware of you silently,
in whom an answer slowly awakens and warms itself
    by listening,
to be the glowing companion of your high-mettled
    feeling.

Oh, and spring would be with you, and never a place
but would give back the music of annunciation.

fragenden Auflaut, den mit steigernder Stille
weithin umschweigt ein reiner, bejahender Tag.
Dann die Stufen hinan, Ruf-Stufen hinan zum
    geträumten
Tempel der Zukunft—; dann den Triller, Fontäne,
die zu dem drängenden Strahl schon das Fallen
    zuvornimmt
im versprechlichen Spiel . . . Und vor sich, den Sommer.
Nicht nur die Morgen alle des Sommers—, nicht nur
wie sie sich wandeln in Tag und strahlen vor Anfang.
Nicht nur die Tage, die zart sind um Blumen, und
    oben,
um die gestalteten Bäume, stark und gewaltig.
Nicht nur die Andacht dieser entfalteten Kräfte,
nicht nur die Wege, nicht nur die Wiesen im Abend,
nicht nur, nach spätem Gewitter, das atmende
    Klarsein,
nicht nur der nahende Schlaf und ein Ahnen,
    abends . . .
sondern die Nächte! Sondern die hohen, des Sommers,
Nächte, sondern die Sterne, die Sterne der Erde.
O einst tot sein und sie wissen unendlich,
alle die Sterne: denn wie, wie, wie sie vergessen!

Siehe, da rief ich die Liebende. Aber nicht *sie* nur
käme . . . Es kämen aus schwächlichen Gräbern
Mädchen und ständen . . . Denn, wie beschränk ich,
wie, den gerufenen Ruf? Die Versunkenen suchen
immer noch Erde.—Ihr Kinder, ein hiesig
einmal ergriffenes Ding gälte für viele.
Glaubt nicht, Schicksal sei mehr als das Dichte der
    Kindheit;

First, that little inquiring outburst, stilled
to increasing silence by a pure yea-saying morning,
far and wide. Then up the stairs (each step a call)
toward the dreamed-of temple of the future;
then the trill, the fountain whose rising jet already
takes the falling water in a game of promise . . .
and before it, the summer. Not only all its mornings,
not only their glowing transformation, radiant with
    beginning.
Not only those days, tender around the flowers, and
    up there,
around the trees, already grown stalwart and strong.
Not only the fervor of these unfolded forces,
not only the pathways, not only the meadows at
    evening,
not only the air with ozone of recent thunderstorm,
not only approaching sleep and a premonition, at
    evening . . .
but the nights! But the lofty nights of summer, but
    the stars,
the stars of earth. Oh, some day to be dead
and to know them forever, all the stars, for how,
how could we forget them!

                    See, I've called the sweetheart.
But not only *she* would come . . . from the weak`
upyielding graves girls would arise and stand . . .
for how could I restrict the call once called?
The sunken are always striving for earth again.—
You children, a thing once grasped here counts for
    many.
Never believe fate's more than the condensation of
    childhood;

wie überholtet ihr oft den Geliebten, atmend,
atmend nach seligem Lauf, auf nichts zu, ins Freie.

Hiersein ist herrlich. Ihr wußtet es, Mädchen, *ihr* auch,
die ihr scheinbar entbehrtet, versankt—, ihr, in den
   ärgsten
Gassen der Städte, Schwärende, oder dem Abfall
Offene. Denn eine Stunde war jeder, vielleicht nicht
ganz eine Stunde, ein mit den Maßen der Zeit kaum
Meßliches zwischen zwei Weilen—, da sie ein Dasein
hatte. Alles. Die Adern voll Dasein.
Nur, wir vergessen so leicht, was der lachende Nachbar
uns nicht bestätigt oder beneidet. Sichtbar
wollen wirs heben, wo doch das sichtbarste Glück uns
erst zu erkennen sich gibt, wenn wir es innen
   verwandeln.

Nirgends, Geliebte, wird Welt sein, als innen. Unser
Leben geht hin mit Verwandlung. Und immer geringer
schwindet das Außen. Wo einmal ein dauerndes Haus
   war,
schlägt sich erdachtes Gebild vor, quer, zu Erdenkli-
   chem
völlig gehörig, als ständ es noch ganz im Gehirne.
Weite Speicher der Kraft schafft sich der Zeitgeist,
   gestaltlos
wie der Spannende Drang, den er aus allem gewinnt.
Tempel kennt er nicht mehr. Diese, des Herzens,
   Verschwendung
sparen wir heimlicher ein. Ja, wo noch eins übersteht,
ein einst gebetetes Ding, ein gedientes, gekknietes—,
hält es sich, so wie es ist, schon ins Unsichtbare hin.
Viele gewahrens nicht mehr, doch ohne den Vorteil,

how often you overtook the beloved, panting,
breathing hard from the blissful chase after nothing,
    but into the open.

To be here is glorious. Girls, you know that, too,
you who missed out, it seems, and sank
in the most infamous alleys of cities, festering,
or open for sewage. But there was an hour for each,
maybe not a whole hour, but a spell between
two whiles, not quite to be measured by meters of time,
when she existed. Completely. Her veins full of being.
But so easily we forget what the laughing neighbor
neither sanctions nor envies. We would exalt
it visibly, although the most visible joy
shows itself to us only when we transmute it, within.

Nowhere, beloved, can world exist but within.
Our life is spent in changing. And ever lessening,
the outer world disappears. Where once was a durable
    house
pops up a fantastic image, crosswise, belonging
    completely
to the conceivable, as though it stood whole in the
    brain.
The spirit of the times makes vast storehouses of power,
formless as the stretched tension it gathers from
    everything.
Temples it knows no longer. We hoard these heart-
    squanderings
more secretly. Yes, where one still lasts, a thing once
for prayer and devotion and kneeling, it holds its own,
as it is, already in the invisible world.
Many can see it no longer and pass up the profit

daß sie's nun *innerlich* baun, mit Pfeilern und
  Statuen, größer!

Jede dumpfe Umkehr der Welt hat solche Enterbte,
denen das Frühere nicht und noch nicht das Nächste
  gehört.
Denn auch das Nächste ist weit für die Menschen.
  Uns soll
dies nicht verwirren; es stärke in uns die Bewahrung
der noch erkannten Gestalt. Dies *stand* einmal unter
  Menschen,
mitten im Schicksal stands, im vernichtenden, mitten
im Nichtwissen-Wohin stand es, wie seiend, und bog
Sterne zu sich aus gesicherten Himmeln. Engel,
dir noch zeig ich es, *da!* in deinem Anschaun
steh es gerettet zuletzt, nun endlich aufrecht.
Säulen, Pylone, der Sphinx, das strebende Stemmen,
grau aus vergehender Stadt oder aus fremder, des Doms.

War es nicht Wunder? O staune, Engel, denn *wir*
  sinds,
wir, o du Großer, erzähls, daß wir solches vermochten,
  mein Atem
reicht für die Rühmung nicht aus. So haben wir
  dennoch
nicht die Räume versäumt, diese gewährenden, diese,
unseren Räume. (Was müssen sie fürchterlich groß
  sein,
da sie Jahrtausende nicht unseres Fühlns überfülln.)
Aber ein Turm war groß, nicht wahr? O Engel, er
  war es,—
groß, auch noch neben dir? Chartres war groß—,
  und Musik

of building it now *within*, with pillars and statues,
  greater!

Each sluggish turn of the world has such disinherited,
to whom belongs neither what's been nor what's
  coming next.
For even the nearest things are far for mortals. This
  ought not
confuse us; it should strengthen us to preserve
the still recognizable form. This *stood* once among
  men,
stood in the middle of fate, the annihilator,
in the center of Not-knowing-whither, as if it existed,
and bent the stars from the established skies
toward it. I show it you, angel, still *there*.
Stand, rescued at last, in your gaze, and finally upright.
Columns, pylons, the Sphinx, the upward striving
of the cathedral, gray, from a foreign or dying city.

Was it not miracle? Oh, marvel, angel, because
it is *we*, O mighty one, we; announce that we did it,
I've not breath enough to hold out for such praising.
So then, we haven't neglected these spaces of *ours*.
(How terribly vast they must be if thousands of years
of our feeling have not overfilled them.) But a tower
  was tall,
was it not? O angel, it was that—great, even beside
  you?
Chartres was great—and music reached still farther
  upward

reichte noch weiter hinan und überstieg uns. Doch
  selbst nur
eine Liebende —, o, allein am nächtlichen Fenster...
reichte sie dir nicht ans Knie—?

                    Glaub *nicht*, daß ich werbe.
Engel, und würb ich dich auch! Du kommst nicht.
  Denn mein
Anruf ist immer voll Hinweg; wider so starke
Strömung kannst du nicht schreiten. Wie ein
  gestreckter
Arm ist mein Rufen. Und seine zum Greifen
oben offene Hand bleibt vor dir
offen, wie Abwehr und Warnung,
Unfaßlicher, weit auf.

and soared beyond us. But even one loving girl,
alone at night, by the window . . .
didn't she reach to your knee?

                    Don't think I am wooing.
Angel, and, if I were, you wouldn't come.
For my appeal is always full of refusal.
You cannot stride against so strong a flood.
Like an outstretched arm is my call. And its grasping
upward open hand stays before you,
open, as safeguard and warning,
you unseizable one, wide open.

Die Achte Elegie

Rudolf Kassner zugeeignet

Mit allen Augen sieht die Kreatur
das Offene. Nur unsre Augen sind
wie umgekehrt und ganz um sie gestellt
als Fallen, rings um ihren freien Ausgang.
Was draußen ist, wir wissens aus des Tiers
Antlitz allein; denn schon das frühe Kind
wenden wir um und zwingens, daß es rückwärts
Gestaltung sehe, nicht das Offne, das
im Tiergesicht so tief ist. Frei von Tod.
Ihn sehen wir allein; das freie Tier
hat seinen Untergang stets hinter sich
und vor sich Gott, und wenn es geht, so gehts
in Ewigkeit, so wie die Brunnen gehen.
Wir haben nie, nicht einen einzigen Tag,
den reinen Raum vor uns, in den die Blumen
unendlich aufgehn. Immer ist es Welt
und niemals Nirgends ohne Nicht:
das Reine, Unüberwachte, das man atmet und
unendlich *weiß* und nicht begehrt. Als Kind
verliert sich eins im stilln an dies und wird

The Eighth Elegy

With full gaze the animal sees the open.
Only our eyes, as if reversed, are like snares
set around it, block the freedom of its going.
Only from the face of the beast do we know
what *is* outside; for even little children
we turn around and force them to look backward
at the world of forms, and they do not see the open
so deep in the animal's eyes. Free from death.
Only we see *that*; but the beast is free
and has its death always behind it and God before it,
and when it walks it goes toward eternity,
as springs flow. Never, not for a single day
do we have pure space before us in which the flowers
are always unfolding. It's forever world
and never Nowhere-without-Not:
the pure and unwatched-over air we breathe,
know infinitely and do not want. As when sometimes
a child gets lost in the silence

gerüttelt. Oder jener stirbt und *ists*.
Denn nah am Tod sieht man den Tod nicht mehr
und starrt *hinaus*, vielleicht mit großem Tierblick.
Liebende, wäre nicht der andre, der
die Sicht verstellt, sind nah daran und staunen . . .
Wie aus Versehn ist ihnen aufgetan
hinter dem andern . . . Aber über ihn
kommt keiner fort, und wieder wird ihm Welt.
Der Schöpfung immer zugewendet, sehn
wir nur auf ihr die Spiegelung des Frei'n,
von uns verdunkelt. Oder daß ein Tier,
ein stummes, aufschaut, ruhig durch uns durch.
Dieses heißt Schicksal: gegenüber sein
und nichts als das und immer gegenüber.

Wäre Bewußtheit unsrer Art in dem
sicheren Tier, das uns entgegenzieht
in anderer Richtung—, riß es uns herum
mit seinem Wandel. Doch sein Sein ist ihm
unendlich, ungefaßt und ohne Blick
auf seinen Zustand, rein, so wie sein Ausblick.
Und wo wir Zukunft sehn, dort sieht es alles
und sich in allem und geheilt für immer.

Und doch ist in dem wachsam warmen Tier
Gewicht und Sorge einer großen Schwermut.
Denn ihm auch haftet immer an, was uns
oft überwältigt,—die Erinnerung,
als sei schon einmal das, wonach man drängt,
näher gewesen, treuer und sein Anschluß
unendlich zärtlich. Hier ist alles Abstand,
und dort wars Atem. Nach der ersten Heimat
ist ihm die zweite zwitterig und windig.
O Seligkeit der *kleinen* Kreatur,

and has to be shaken back. Or someone dies and *is it*.
For nearing death, one sees death no more and stares
   forward,
perhaps with the wide gaze of the animal.
Lovers, were it not for the other who blocks the view,
are close to it and marvel . . .
as if by carelessness it is open to them
behind each other . . . but neither gets past, and again
it's world. Always turned to creation, we see there
only the reflection of the free,
darkened by us. Or that a beast, a dumb one,
lifts his eyes and looks us calmly through and through.
That's what Destiny is: to be face to face
and nothing but that and always opposite.

If the sure animal that approaches us
in a different direction had this awareness of ours,
he would drag us along behind him. But his existence
is infinite to him, ungrasped, without a glimpse
at his condition, pure as his outward gaze.
And where we see the future, he sees All
and himself in All and himself healed forever.

And yet within the warm and watchful creature
is the care and heaviness of a great melancholy.
For it also clings to him always, that
which often overcomes us—memory:
as if once before the thing for which we strive
had been closer, truer, and the relation
infinitely tender. Here all is distance,
there it was breath. After the first home
the second is hybrid and open to the winds.
Oh, the beatitude of the *little* creatures

die immer *bleibt* im Schooße, der sie austrug;
o Glück der Mücke, die noch *innen* hüpft,
selbst wenn sie Hochzeit hat: denn Schooß ist alles.
Und sieh die halbe Sicherheit des Vogels,
der beinah beides weiß aus seinem Ursprung,
als wär er eine Seele der Etrusker,
aus einem Toten, den ein Raum empfing,
doch mit der ruhenden Figur als Deckel.
Und wie bestürzt ist eins, das fliegen muß
und stammt aus einem Schooß. Wie vor sich selbst
erschreckt, durchzuckts die Luft, wie wenn ein Sprung
durch eine Tasse geht. So reißt die Spur
der Fledermaus durchs Porzellan des Abends.

Und wir, Zuschauer, immer, überall,
dem allen zugewandt und nie hinaus!
Uns überfüllts. Wir ordnens. Es zerfällt.
Wir ordnens wieder und zerfallen selbst.

Wer hat uns also umgedreht, daß wir,
was wir auch tun, in jener Haltung sind
von einem, welcher fortgeht? Wie er auf
dem letzten Hügel, der ihm ganz sein Tal
noch einmal zeigt, sich wendet, anhält, weilt—,
so leben wir und nehmen immer Abschied.

that *stay* forever in the womb that conceived them;
oh, the joy of the midge that is still hopping *within*,
even during its nuptials: for womb is all.
And look at the half-certainty of the bird
that from its origin knows almost both;
as if it were the soul of a dead Etruscan
shut in the space where his effigy rests as a lid.
And how perturbed is anything come from a womb
when it has to fly! As if afraid of itself,
it jerks through the air, as a crack goes through a cup.
As the track of a bat tears through the porcelain of
    evening.

And we: onlookers, always, everywhere,
turned toward everything and never from!
We are surfeited. We set it in order. It breaks.
We put it in order again and break down ourselves.

Who has twisted us like this, so that—
no matter what we do—we have the bearing
of a man going away? As on the last hill
that shows him all his valley, for the last time,
he turns, stands still, and lingers, so we live,
forever saying farewell.

Die Neunte Elegie

Warum, wenn es angeht, also die Frist des Daseins
hinzubringen, als Lorbeer, ein wenig dunkler als alles
andere Grün, mit kleinen Wellen an jedem
Blattrand (wie eines Windes Lächeln)—: warum dann
Menschliches müssen—und, Schicksal vermeidend,
sich sehnen nach Schicksal? ...

                   O, *nicht*, weil Glück *ist*
dieser voreilige Vorteil eines nahen Verlusts.
Nicht aus Neugier, oder zur Übung des Herzens,
das auch im Lorbeer *wäre* ...
Aber weil Hiersein viel ist, und weil uns scheinbar
alles das Hiesige braucht, dieses Schwindende, das
seltsam uns angeht. Uns, die Schwindendsten. *Ein* Mal
jedes, nur *ein* Mal. *Ein* Mal und nicht mehr. Und wir
    auch
ein Mal. Nie wieder. Aber dieses
ein Mal gewesen zu sein, wenn auch nur *ein* Mal:
irdisch gewesen zu sein, scheint nicht widerrufbar.

Und so drängen wir uns und wollen es leisten,

The Ninth Elegy

Why, if it's possible to spend this span
of existence as laurel, a little darker than all
other greens, with little waves on every
leaf-edge (like the smile of a breeze), why, then,
must we be human and, shunning destiny,
long for it? ...

              Oh, not because happiness,
that over-hasty profit of loss impending, *exists*.
Not from curiosity, or to practise the heart,
that would also be in the laurel ...
but because to be here is much, and the transient Here
seems to need and concern us strangely. Us, the most
    transient.
Everyone *once*, *once* only. Just *once* and no more.
And we also *once*. Never again. But this having been
once, although only *once*, to have been of the earth,
seems irrevocable.

And so we drive ourselves and want to achieve it,

wollens enthalten in unsern einfachen Händen,
im überfüllteren Blick und im sprachlosen Herzen.
Wollen es werden. Wem es geben? Am liebsten
alles behalten für immer . . . Ach, in den andern Bezug,
wehe, was nimmt man hinüber? Nicht das Anschaun,
     das hier
langsam erlernte, und kein hier Ereignetes. Keins.
Also die Schmerzen. Also vor allem das Schwersein,
also der Liebe lange Erfahrung,—also
lauter Unsägliches. Aber später,
unter den Sternen, was solls: *die* sind *besser* unsäglich.
Bringt doch der Wanderer auch vom Hange des
     Bergrands
nicht eine Hand voll Erde ins Tal, die allen unsägliche,
     sondern
ein erworbenes Wort, reines, den gelben und blaun
Enzian. Sind wir vielleicht *hier,* um zu sagen: Haus,
Brücke, Brunnen, Tor, Krug, Obstbaum, Fenster,—
höchstens: Säule, Turm . . . aber zu *sagen,* verstehs,
o zu sagen *so,* wie selber die Dinge niemals
innig meinten zu sein. Ist nicht die heimliche List
dieser verschwiegenen Erde, wenn sie die Liebenden
     drängt,
daß sich in ihrem Gefühl jedes und jedes entzückt?
Schwelle: was ists für zwei
Liebende, daß sie die eigne ältere Schwelle der Tür
ein wenig verbrauchen, auch sie, nach den vielen vorher
und vor den künftigen . . . , leicht.

Hier ist des *Säglichen* Zeit, *hier* seine Heimat.
Sprich und bekenn. Mehr als je
fallen die Dinge dahin, die erlebbaren, denn,
was sie verdrängend ersetzt, ist ein Tun ohne Bild,
Tun unter Krusten, die willig zerspringen, sobald

want to hold it in our simple hands,
in the surfeited gaze and in the speechless heart.
Want to become it. Give it to whom? Rather
keep all forever . . . but to the other realm,
alas, what can be taken? Not the power of seeing,
learned here so slowly, and nothing that's happened
    here.
Nothing. Maybe the suffering? Before all, the heaviness
and long experience of love—unutterable things.
But later, under the stars, what then? *They* are *better*
    untold of.
The wanderer does not bring a handful of earth,
the unutterable, from the mountain slope to the valley,
but a pure word he has learned, the blue
and yellow gentian. Are we *here* perhaps just to say:
house, bridge, well, gate, jug, fruit tree, window—
at most, column, tower . . . but to *say*, understand this,
    to say it
as the Things themselves never fervently thought to be.
Is it not the hidden cunning of secretive earth
when it urges on the lovers, that everything seems
    transfigured
in their feelings? Threshold, what is it for two lovers
that they wear away a little of their own older doorsill,
they also, after the many before,
and before those yet coming . . . lightly?

Here is the time for the *unutterable, here,* its country.
Speak and acknowledge it. More than ever
the things that we can live by are falling away,
supplanted by an action without symbol.
An action beneath crusts that easily crack, as soon as

innen das Handeln entwächst und sich anders
   begrenzt.
Zwischen den Hämmern besteht
unser Herz, wie die Zunge
zwischen den Zähnen, die doch,
dennoch die preisende bleibt.

Preise dem Engel die Welt, nicht die unsägliche, ihm
kannst du nicht großtun mit herrlich Erfühltem; im
   Weltall,
wo er fühlender fühlt, bist du ein Neuling, drum zeig
ihm das Einfache, das, von Geschlecht zu
   Geschlechtern gestaltet,
als ein Unsriges lebt neben der Hand und im Blick.
Sag ihm die Dinge. Er wird staunender stehn; wie du
   standest
bei dem Seiler in Rom, oder beim Töpfer am Nil.
Zeig ihm, wie glücklich ein Ding sein kann, wie
   schuldlos und unser,
wie selbst das klagende Leid rein zur Gestalt sich
   entschließt,
dient als ein Ding, oder stirbt in ein Ding—, und
   jenseits
selig der Geige entgeht. Und diese, von Hingang
lebenden Dinge verstehn, daß du sie rühmst;
   vergänglich,
traun sie ein Rettendes uns, den Vergänglichsten, zu.
Wollen, wir sollen sie ganz im unsichtbarn Herzen
   verwandeln
in—o unendlich—in uns! wer wir am Ende auch seien.

Erde, ist es nicht dies, was du willst: *unsichtbar*
in uns erstehn?—Ist es dein Traum nicht,
einmal unsichtbar zu sein?—Erde! unsichtbar!

the inner working outgrows and otherwise limits itself.
Our heart exists between hammers,
like the tongue between the teeth,
but notwithstanding, the tongue
always remains the praiser.

Praise the world to the angel, not the unutterable
    world;
you cannot astonish him with your glorious feelings;
in the universe, where he feels more sensitively,
you're just a beginner. Therefore, show him the simple
thing that is shaped in passing from father to son,
that lives near our hands and eyes as our very own.
Tell him about the Things. He'll stand more amazed,
    as you stood
beside the rope-maker in Rome, or the potter on the
    Nile.
Show him how happy a thing can be, how blameless
    and ours;
how even the lamentation of sorrow purely decides
to take form, serves as a thing, or dies
in a thing, and blissfully in the beyond
escapes the violin. And these things that live,
slipping away, understand that you praise them;
transitory themselves, they trust us for rescue,
us, the most transient of all. They wish us to
    transmute them
in our invisible heart—oh, infinitely into us!
    Whoever we are.

Earth, isn't this what you want: *invisibly*
to arise in us? Is it not your dream
to be some day invisible? Earth! Invisible!

Was, wenn Verwandlung nicht, ist dein drängender
  Auftrag?
Erde, du liebe, ich will. O glaub, es bedürfte
nicht deiner Frühlinge mehr, mich dir zu gewinnen—,
  einer,
ach, ein einziger ist schon dem Blute zu viel.
Namenlos bin ich zu dir entschlossen, von weit her.
Immer warst du im Recht, und dein heiliger Einfall
ist der vertrauliche Tod.
Siehe, ich lebe. Woraus? Weder Kindheit noch Zukunft
werden weniger . . . Überzähliges Dasein
entspringt mir im Herzen.

What, if not transformation, is your insistent
    commission?
Earth, dear one, I will! Oh, believe it needs
not one more of your springtimes to win me over.
One, just one, is already too much for my blood.
From afar I'm utterly determined to be yours.
You were always right and your sacred revelation
    is the intimate death.
Behold, I'm alive. On what? Neither childhood nor
    future
grows less . . . surplus of existence
is welling up in my heart.

Die Zehnte Elegie

Dass ich dereinst, an dem Ausgang der grimmigen
   Einsicht,
Jubel und Ruhm aufsinge zustimmenden Engeln.
Daß von den klargeschlagenen Hämmern des Herzens
keiner versage an weichen, zweifelnden oder
reißenden Saiten. Daß mich mein strömendes Antlitz
glänzender mache: daß das unscheinbare Weinen
blühe. O wie werdet ihr dann, Nächte, mir lieb sein,
gehärmte. Daß ich euch knieender nicht, untröstliche
   Schwestern,
hinnahm, nicht in euer gelöstes
Haar mich gelöster ergab. Wir, Vergeuder der
   Schmerzen.
Wie wir sie absehn voraus, in die traurige Dauer,
ob sie nicht enden vielleicht. Sie aber sind ja
unser winterwähriges Laub, unser dunkeles Sinngrün,
eine der Zeiten des heimlichen Jahres—, nicht nur
Zeit—, sind Stelle, Siedelung, Lager, Boden, Wohnort.

The Tenth Elegy

May I some day, at the exit of grim understanding,
sing out jubilation and praise to affirmative angels!
May none of the clear-struck hammers of the heart
fall on loose, uncertain, or breaking strings.
May my streaming face make me more shining. May
   humble weeping
bloom. O nights, how dear you will be to me then,
nights of grieving. Alas, that I did not on my knees,
   kneeling more,
accept you, more yielding lose myself, disconsolate
   sisters,
in your loosened hair. We, spendthrifts of the sorrows.
How we stare ahead of them into mournful duration,
to see if maybe they'll end. But they are really only
our winter-hardy foliage, our dusky evergreen,
one of the seasons of our secret year—not only a
   season,
but place, settlement, camp, grounds, habitation.

Freilich, wehe, wie fremd sind die Gassen der
    Leid-Stadt,
wo in der falschen, aus Übertönung gemachten
Stille, stark, aus der Gußform des Leeren der Ausguß,
prahlt der vergoldete Lärm, das platzende Denkmal.
O, wie spurlos zerträte ein Engel ihnen den Trostmarkt,
den die Kirche begrenzt, ihre fertig gekaufte:
reinlich und zu und enttäuscht wie ein Postamt am
    Sonntag.
Draußen aber kräuseln sich immer die Ränder von
    Jahrmarkt.
Schaukeln der Freiheit! Taucher und Gaukler des
    Eifers!
Und des behübschten Glücks figürliche Schießstatt,
wo es zappelt von Ziel und sich blechern benimmt,
wenn ein Geschickterer trifft. Von Beifall zu Zufall
taumelt er weiter; denn Buden jeglicher Neugier
werben, trommeln und plärrn. Für Erwachsene aber
ist noch besonders zu sehn, wie das Geld sich
    vermehrt, anatomisch,
nicht zur Belustigung nur: der Geschlechtsteil des
    Gelds,
alles, das Ganze, der Vorgang—, das unterrichtet
    und macht
fruchtbar . . .
. . . O aber gleich darüber hinaus,
hinter der letzten Planke, beklebt mit Plakaten des
    „Todlos",
jenes bitteren Biers, das den Trinkenden süß scheint,
wenn sie immer dazu frische Zerstreuungen kau'n . . . ,
gleich im Rücken der Planke, gleich dahinter, ists
    wirklich.

Yes, and alas, how strange are the streets of the
    City of Pain,
where in the false silence made out of uproar's
    resounding,
violent, a casting from the mold of vacuum, blusters
the gilded hubbub, the blurting monument.
Oh, how an angel would trample—and leave no
    trace—
their marketplace of solace, with the church on the
    edge,
bought ready-made: clean and disappointed
and closed tight as the post office on Sunday.
But always out there are frizzling the borders of the
    yearly fair.
Seesaws of freedom! High-divers and jugglers of petty
    zeal.
The symbolical shooting-gallery of flashy luck,
where the tin targets jerk and rattle when a crack shot
    hits them.
From applause to chance he staggers, for the booths
    are coaxing
all the curious with drums and barkers' bawling.
But for the adults there's something special to see:
How Money Propagates! Anatomical—not for
    amusement only!
The genitals of Money! All, complete, the Act!
It instructs and makes you prolific! . . .
. . . Oh, but just outside, behind the last billboard,
    pasted
with posters of "Deathless," that bitter beer that tastes
so sweet to the drinkers, if they chew fresh diversions
    with it . . .
but just behind the billboard, just back of it,
    everything's *real*.

Kinder spielen, und Liebende halten einander abseits,
ernst, im ärmlichen Gras, und Hunde haben Natur.
Weiter noch zieht es den Jüngling; vielleicht, daß er
     eine junge
Klage liebt ... Hinter ihr her kommt er in Wiesen.
     Sie sagt:
Weit. Wir wohnen dort draußen ...
                                        Wo? Und der Jüngling
folgt. Ihn rührt ihre Haltung. Die Schulter, der
     Hals—, vielleicht
ist sie von herrlicher Herkunft. Aber er läßt sie,
     kehrt um,
wendet sich, winkt ... Was solls? Sie ist eine Klage.

Nur die jungen Toten, im ersten Zustand
zeitlosen Gleichmuts, dem der Entwöhnung,
folgen ihr liebend. Mädchen
wartet sie ab und befreundet sie. Zeigt ihnen leise,
was sie an sich hat. Perlen des Leids und die feinen
Schleier der Duldung.—Mit Jünglingen geht sie
schweigend.

Aber dort, wo sie wohnen, im Tal, der älteren eine
     der Klagen
nimmt sich des Jünglings an, wenn er fragt:—Wir
     waren,
sagt sie, ein großes Geschlecht, einmal, wir Klagen.
     Die Väter
trieben den Bergbau dort in dem großen Gebirg; bei
     Menschen
findest du manchmal ein Stück geschliffenes Urleid
oder, aus altem Vulkan, schlackig versteinerten Zorn.
Ja, das stammte von dort. Einst waren wir reich.—

Children play and the lovers are embracing each
    other—aside there,
seriously, on the sorry grass, the dogs answer nature.
Farther the young man is lured; perhaps by love for a
    young
Lament . . . he follows her into the meadow. She says:
    It's far.
We live out yonder . . .
                    Where? And the young man follows,
stirred by her bearing. The shoulders, the neck—
    maybe she comes
of noble stock. But he leaves her, turns back, looks
    around,
waves . . . But what's the use? She's just a Lament.

Only those who died young, in their first state
of timeless serenity, when they are being weaned,
follow her, lovingly. She waits for
girls and befriends them. Gently she shows them
what she is wearing. Pearls of suffering and the fine
veils of patience.—With young men she walks in
    silence.

But there, where they dwell in the valley, one of the
    older Laments
listens to him when he questions:—We were once,
    she says, a great
family, we Laments. The fathers
worked the mines in those mountains; among men
often you'll find a shard of polished primeval pain,
or the petrified slag of anger from an old volcano.
Yes, that came from up there. We used to be rich.—

Und sie leitet ihn leicht durch die weite Landschaft
    der Klagen,
zeigt ihm die Säulen der Tempel oder die Trümmer
jener Burgen, von wo Klage-Fürsten das Land
einstens weise beherrscht. Zeigt ihm die hohen
Tränenbäume und Felder blühender Wehmut,
(Lebendige kennen sie nur als sanftes Blattwerk);
zeigt ihm die Tiere der Trauer, weidend,—und
    manchmal
schreckt ein Vogel und zieht, flach ihnen fliegend
    durchs Aufschaun,
weithin das schriftliche Bild seines vereinsamten
    Schreis.—
Abends führt sie ihn hin zu den Gräbern der Alten
aus dem Klage-Geschlecht, den Sibyllen und
    Warn-Herrn.
Naht aber Nacht, so wandeln sie leiser, und bald
mondets empor, das über alles
wachende Grab-Mal. Brüderlich jenem am Nil,
der erhabene Sphinx—: der verschwiegenen Kammer
Antlitz.
Und sie staunen dem krönlichen Haupt, das für immer,
schweigend, der Menschen Gesicht
auf die Wage der Sterne gelegt.

Nicht erfaßt es sein Blick, im Frühtod
schwindelnd. Aber ihr Schaun,
hinter dem Pschent-Rand hervor, scheucht es die
    Eule. Und sie,
streifend im langsamen Abstrich die Wange entlang,

Then lightly she leads him through the broad
    countryside of the Sorrows,
shows him the columns of temples or the ruins
of those strongholds from which the princes of
    Lamentation
wisely ruled the country, once upon a time.
Shows him the tall trees of tears and fields of
    blossoming sadness
(the living know these only as tender foliage);
shows him the beasts of mourning as they graze;
and sometimes a bird is frightened and straight
    through the field of their vision
trails the written image of its isolated cry.—
At evening she takes him out to the graves of the elders
of the race of Lamentation, the sibyls and prophets.
But when night falls, they walk more slowly, and soon
the sepulcher that overwatches all
moons upward. Brother to him on the Nile,
the exalted Sphinx: the face of the secret chamber.*
And they marvel at the royal head, that forever
silently laid the features of man
on the scales of the stars.**

Dizzy from just having died, his sight
cannot grasp it. But her gaze
scares out an owl from the rim of the double crown.***
Brushing with slow downstrokes along the cheek,

* The *mastaba*, a building that stands before the pyramid.
** The constellation Libra.
*** The double crown was the *pschent*, the united crowns
of Upper and Lower Egypt.

jene der reifesten Rundung,
zeichnet weich in das neue
Totengehör, über ein doppelt
aufgeschlagenes Blatt, den unbeschreiblichen Umriß.

Und höher, die Sterne. Neue. Die Sterne des Leidlands.
Langsam nennt sie die Klage: „Hier,
siehe: den *Reiter*, den *Stab*, und das vollere Sternbild
nennen sie: *Fruchtkranz*. Dann, weiter, dem Pol zu:
Wiege; Weg; Das brennende Buch; Puppe; Fenster.
Aber im südlichen Himmel, rein wie im Innern
einer gesegneten Hand, das Klar erglänzende ‚M‘,
das die Mütter bedeutet . . . "

Doch der Tote muß fort, und schweigend bringt ihn
    die ältere
Klage bis an die Talschlucht,
wo es schimmert im Mondschein:
die Quelle der Freude. In Ehrfurcht
nennt sie sie, sagt:—Bei den Menschen
ist sie ein tragender Strom.—

Stehn am Fuß des Gebirgs.
Und da umarmt sie ihn, weinend.

Einsam steigt er dahin, in die Berge des Ur-Leids,
Und nicht einmal sein Schritt klingt aus dem
    tonlosen Los.

on its ripest roundness, faintly the bird
traces on the new hearing of the dead,
on the two pages of an open book,
the indescribable contour.

And higher, the stars, the new ones. The stars of the
    land of Sorrow.
Slowly the Lament names them: "See there—
The *Rider*, the *Staff*, and that crowded constellation
is called the *Garland of Fruit*. Then farther, toward
    the Pole:
Cradle, Road, the Burning Book, Doll, Window.
But in the southern sky, pure as if cupped
in a blessed hand, the brightly shining *M*,
that stands for the Mothers . . ." *

But the dead man must go on, and silently the elder
Lament takes him to the gorge
where shimmers in moonlight
the springhead of joy. She names it
with reverence, saying: "In the world of men
this is a ship-bearing river."

They stand at the foot of the mountain.
And there she embraces him, weeping.

Lonely, he climbs the mountains of primeval pain.
And never once does his footstep ring from this
    soundless doom.

* This arbitrary astronomical nomenclature is best regarded
as obvious symbolism. These are the "Things" so dear to
Rilke. Had the M been in the north, it would be Cassiopeia's
Chair. The idea of the Mothers comes from *Faust*, Part II,
where they are the guardians of the archetypes.

Aber erweckten sie uns, die unendlich Toten, ein
    Gleichnis,
siehe, sie zeigten vielleicht auf die Kätzchen der leeren
Hasel, die hängenden, oder
meinten den Regen, der fällt auf dunkles Erdreich
    im Frühjahr.—

Und wir, die an *steigendes* Glück
denken, empfänden die Rührung,
die uns beinah bestürzt,
wenn ein Glückliches *fällt*.

Yet, if they awakened a symbol within us, these
   endlessly
dead, look, they'd point at the catkins
that hang on the leafless hazels, or maybe they'd **mean**
the rain that falls on black earth in the early spring.—

Then we, who think of *rising* happiness,
would feel the emotion
that almost confounds us
when a happy Thing *falls*.

Bibliography

Andreas-Salomé, Lou. *Rainer Maria Rilke*. Leipzig: Insel-Verlag, 1928.

Angelloz, J.-F. *Rainer Maria Rilke. L'Évolution spirituelle du poète*. Paris: P. Hartmann, 1936.

———. *Rainer Maria Rilke. Les Élégies de Duino. Suivi de: Les Sonnets à Orphée*. Traduits et préfacés. Paris: Aubier, 1943.

———. *Rilke*. Paris: Mercure de France, 1952.

Arendt, Hannah, and Gunther Stern. "Rilkes Duineser Elegien," *Neue Schweizer Rundschau*, November, 1930.

Besserman, Dieter. *Der späte Rilke*. München: R. Oldenbourg, 1947.

Borris, Norbert. "Tier, Mensch und Engle bei R. M. Rilke," *Die Schildgenossen*, July-August, 1929.

Brecht, Franz Josef. *Schicksal und Auftrag des Menschen. Philosophische Interpretation zu Rilkes Duineser Elegien*. Basel: E. Reinhardt, 1949.

Cämmerer, Heinrich. *Rainer Maria Rilkes Duineser Elegien: Deutung der Dichtung*. Stuttgart: J. B. Metzlersche Verlagsbuchhandlung, 1937.

Cassirer-Solmitz, Eva. *Rainer Maria Rilke*. Heidelberg: G. Koester, 1957.

Goertz, Hartmann. *Frankreich und das Erlebnis der Form im Werke Rainer Maria Rilkes*. Stuttgart: J. B. Metzlersche Verlagsbuchhandlung, 1932.

Graff, W. L. *Rainer Maria Rilke: Creative Anguish of a Modern Poet*. Princeton: Princeton University Press, 1956.

Guardini, Romano. *Zu Rainer Maria Rilkes Deutung des Daseins: Eine Interpretation d. 2., 8. u. 9. Duineser Elegie*. München: Kösel-Verlag, 1953.

Gundolf, Friedrich. *Rainer Maria Rilke*. Wien: Verlag der Johannespresse, 1937.

Günther, Werner. *Weltinnenraum. Die Dichtung Rainer Maria Rilkes*. Berlin: Haupt, 1943.

Holthusen, Hans-Egon. *Rilkes Sonette an Orpheus. Versuch einer Interpretation*. München: Neuer Filser-Verlag, 1937.

Kaubisch, Martin. *Rainer Maria Rilke. Mystik und Künstlertum*. Dresden: Jess, 1936.

Kaufmann, Fritz. *Sprache als Schöpfung. Zur absoluten Kunst in Hinblick auf Rilke*. Stuttgart: Enke, 1934.

Kippenberg, Katharine. *Rainer Maria Rilkes Duineser Elegien und Sonette an Orpheus*. Leipzig: Insel-Verlag, 1948.

Klatt, Fritz. *Rainer Maria Rilke*. Wien: Amandus-Edition, 1948.

———. *Sieg über die Angst: Die Weltangst des modernen Menschen und ihre Überwindung durch Rainer Maria Rilke*. Berlin: L. Schneider, 1940.

Kreutz, Heinrich. *Rilkes Duineser Elegien: Eine Interpretation*. München: C. H. Beck'sche Verlagsbuchhandlung, 1950.

Mason, Eudo C. *Lebenshaltung und Symbolik bei Rainer Maria Rilke*. Weimar: Böhlaus, 1939.

———. *Rilke: Europe and the English-speaking World*. London: Cambridge University Press, 1961.

Petersen, Jürgen. *Das Todesproblem bei Rainer Maria Rilke*. Würzburg: Triltsch, 1936.

Salis, J. R. von. *Rainer Maria Rilkes Schweizer Jahre*. Frauenfeld-Leipzig: Hüber, 1952.

Schmidt-Pauli, Elisabeth von. *Hiersein ist herrlich: Erläuterungen zu Rainer Maria Rilkes Duineser Elegien*. Konstanz-Nussdorf: Internationaler Verlag, 1948.

Sieber, Karl. *René Rilke. Die Jugend Rainer Maria Rilkes*. Leipzig: Insel-Verlag, 1932.

Trapp, Arnold. *Rainer Maria Rilkes Duineser Elegien*. Diss. Giessen; 1936.

Vietta, Egon. "Ueber die Duineser Elegien," *Neue Rund-schau*, December, 1936.

Wolf, Werner. *Rainer Maria Rilkes Duineser Elegien. Eine Textbedeutung*. Heidelberg: Carl Winter, 1937.

In addition to the bibliographies appended to my other books of translations from the poet, I wish to acknowledge indebtedness to E. M. Butler's *Rainer Maria Rilke* (New York: Macmillan, 1941); the introduction and commentary to the translation of the *Duino Elegies* by J. B. Leishman and Stephen Spender (3d ed.; London: Hogarth Press, 1948); and, most of all, to E. L. Stahl's "The Duineser Elegien," in *Rainer Maria Rilke: Aspects of His Mind and Poetry*, edited by William Rose and G. Craig Houston (London: Sidgwick & Jackson, 1938).